Jan19
/c
11/20/18
$u = 4$

Children
of
Tomorrow

Guidelines for Raising Happy Children
in the 21st Century

by
MICHAEL LAITMAN

LAITMAN
KABBALAH
PUBLISHERS

Children of Tomorrow
Guidelines for Raising Happy Children in the 21st Century

Printed in Canada

Compilation: S. Ratz, G. Gerchikov, H. Kantzberg, R. Cohen, L. Regev-Gol,
Y. Garanturov, T. Akerman, J. Gamburg, A. Sharabi, H. Tapiaro, A. Adam,
V. Teshuva, M. Ravi, S. Gal, M. Pikler, A. Belotzerkovsky, Y. Kim
Translation: Y. Naor
Copy Editor: C. Gerus
Associate Editors: R.M. Montan, C. Medansky, S.M. Kosinec, B. Shillington
Cover and Layout Design: Studio Yaniv, B. Khovov
Executive Editor: C. Ratz
Publishing and Post Production: Uri Laitman

ISBN 978-1-897448-58-8
Library of Congress Control Number: 2011924002

FIRST EDITION: DECEMBER 2011
First printing

Contents

"We create nothing new.
Our work is only to illuminate
What is hidden within."

Menachem Mendel of Kotzk

Introduction

Introduction

In each of us, there is a spark that calls to us from the deepest place. The hustle and bustle of everyday life may have blurred it in our minds, but each time we look at our children, it slips out of the dark and touches us deep within our hearts. For a fleeting moment, it reminds us that once, long ago, we were different. We had dreams and saw the world through different eyes—simpler, truer, purer, and more penetrating.

Today, a new generation is growing just around the corner, and it is unwilling to settle for what there is, and certainly not for what there was. This generation will not let that spark be put out. It is a generation that wants to know, to understand, and to discover what life is for. And they, our children, will not rest until we bring them something real, something to nourish their hearts.

Children of Tomorrow consists of inspiring yet poignant excerpts, put together from talks that Kabbalist Dr. Michael Laitman held with psychologists, educators, parents, and children. Together, these excerpts offer a taste of a profound, expansive educational method based on the wisdom of Kabbalah, which is intended for this generation.

It is a book that will bring a new light to those whose hearts are keen on education, parents who wish to see a brighter future for their children, teachers and educators who wish to broaden their horizons, and anyone whose heart still feels a tinge of the child within.

PART ONE
A New Generation

CHAPTER ONE
Forging Ahead

Beyond Matter

There will come a generation,
We hope to see it soon,
That will truly crave to break free from this world
Into a world of information,
A world of forces,
Into what lies beyond matter,
And which is called "the spiritual world."

A Need to Be Human

Today
Is the first time
We feel,
While still not understanding,
That the younger generation
Is discovering
A need
To develop
The "human" within.

On a Different Frequency

This generation is special.
It is tuned into a different frequency
Compared to previous generations
Because its receiver is different.

A Special Generation

The younger generation
Is completely different souls,
Of a different quality.

They want to literally
Feel the higher, more spiritual world.
The children of today are built for it.

If we only begin to study with them
We will quickly feel how they are pulling us
Forward, inside,
To the vast realms of the wisdom.

Adapting Ourselves
to the Younger Generation

To touch children's hearts,
We, who come from an older generation,
Must recognize
How fundamentally different we are from them.

We should not think
That they must love
And accept us as we are
Without our changing.

On the contrary,
We must try
To adapt ourselves to them
As much as possible.

Treating Children as Adults

Today's children
Are actually mature
In their internal
Preparation for development,
And we must treat them as such.

Looking for Genuine Joy

Look at the younger generation.
They have everything!
But they are dissatisfied.
Why do they turn to drugs?
Because they don't enjoy a life such as ours.

Generation Disconnect

The renewal of souls in the present generation
Makes the young feel as if
They have nothing to learn from adults.
Indeed, what can they learn from people who tell them:
"Get up in the morning,
Go to work,
Be good,
Marry,
Have kids,
And everything will be OK."

CHAPTER TWO
A New Method

Focus on the Soul

Today's young people need a higher quality of education
· That our current education cannot provide.
Children may be small in size, so "What do they know?"
But it's their souls we must consider.

A Fundamental Change

The younger generation is growing with a global desire.
They belong to a global world.
We can no longer approach them in the old ways,
So we will have to change
Our education system
From the ground up.

Their education must be suitable for the new souls
That are appearing today,
Without coercion,
And with an explanation of man's essence.
Only this approach will succeed.

Explaining Life's Essence

Education does not end with
Teaching behavioral codes.
Rather, education should be
An explanation of life's essence,
The way to realize the qualities of one's soul.

The Problem With Our Education

The problem with our education is
That we are not building children
To become human beings.

We give them knowledge,
But we do not educate them
In the full sense of the word.
To "educate" means to teach children
How to relate to themselves
And to others properly,
To be one, whole human being.

Instead,

We give them technical information:

How to turn a screw, how to work with a computer,

A little bit of science,

And we send them on their way.

We do not teach children

How to live their lives correctly,

Hence we are faced with a truly

Unhappy generation.

Human Crisis

Today people cannot make discoveries in nature because we have divided it into frames and boxes.

We have come to a point where each person is a bolt in a machine, knowing which job to pursue and what to study to make more money. And this is all we strive for.

But the endless pursuit of happiness does not make us happy. On the contrary, we are in crisis in science, education, culture, and every human engagement, precisely because we are not building humans.

Let us hope that the crisis we are in is the beginning of the end of our wrong, and our wrongful attitude toward each other.

Teaching What the Soul Requires

If we give children everything their souls wish to receive today, it is almost certain that hyperactive disorders will disappear.

We must stop "stuffing" them with study subjects inherited from previous generations that they no longer need for life. Instead, we must begin to satisfy their need to develop the soul.

A Whole New Generation
Seeks a Whole New Fulfillment

This is a generation that requires a different fulfillment.

We call this behavior

"Hyperactive disorder,"

But it is not "Hyper,"Only "active."

It is as active

As the needs

Within require.

In Harmony with Their Outbursts

We should restructure the education systems on all levels and for all ages so that children feel good, evolve freely and pleasantly, and live in harmony with their eruptive egos.

We mustn't restrain children. On the contrary, we must find a way to be "in harmony" with their outbursts, their egos, and their energy.

Living in the Dark

We were not brought up to be human beings.
We were never told how we were built:
Our desires,
Our qualities,
What governs us,
Where we have freedom of choice, where we do not.
We were never taught the laws for the collective
And for individuals,
And how they evolve.

We don't know anything
About ourselves
Or about the environment.
This is what our lives look like:
Living in the dark.

Educating Just One Generation Correctly

If we bring up just one generation correctly,
If we give today's children what they need,
Even to a small extent,
They will pass it on to the next generation.

And the next generations
Will no longer be declining,
But ascending.

Otherwise,
The next generation
Will sink into despair and drugs.
What a pity for our children.

Simply Happy

If we bring up children
In the right way,
Ten years from now
We'll see a very different generation.

Children will know
The kind of world they live in
And will understand
The consequences
Of each of their actions.

As a result,
They will build their
Actions,
Thoughts,
Intentions,
And relations
In such a good and proper way
That they will simply
Be happy.

PART TWO
Principles
of Education

CHAPTER ONE

The Environment
Builds the Person

Children of Tomorrow

The environment of children today determines what they will be tomorrow.

This is why we must give them positive examples, make films, write stories, and so forth.

This is the only way children will gradually absorb the examples we wish to convey to them, and those examples, in turn, will form their personalities.

Establishing a Society

The right education means
Establishing around a person
A society that constantly promotes
The right connections
With the environment.

We Are Educated by Our Environment

The most important thing is not the teachers or the textbooks: we are educated by our environment.

Hence, the main thing to build in schools is a good social environment for children where each child feels committed to be a friend and to support the other children in a positive and helpful manner.

Then, our natural qualities—envy, cravings, pursuit of honor, and competitiveness—will only promote children because they will develop sensitivity toward society, and through it they will develop in the right direction.

Only the Environment

Children should be educated by their environment. We needn't even encourage them to participate in discussions, tell them what they should do, or comment on their behavior.

All we need is to help them grow and change in the right way through their environment. The environment is the primary element in our development.

No Violence in Our Schools

We must provide children with the proper foundation to establish the right connection with society, to show them how connected they are to society, how much they are dependent upon it, and how they can influence it.

All cases of outbursts, extreme violence, and terrorism stem from the fact that no one taught these children how to establish proper contact with society.

We often do things that are quite cruel because we don't feel that society is responsive toward us. So it is with those antisocial people—they only want to find their place in society.

Therefore, from the very beginning, we must build for children the right system of connections with society, with the environment. We should build for them a social environment comprised of children who are similar to them, and work with them together so that they understand each other and develop in harmony among them.

If we do that, we will be able to avoid all the negative phenomena that exist in society today.

Environment—the Solution to Hyperactivity

We find it hard to grasp that the ubiquitous hyperactive disorder is not a disease, but a symptom, a result of the absence of the right environment.

We are not giving our children the proper environment in which to develop; this is why they react in such a way. Instead of meeting our children's needs, we suppress their natural need and call it "hyperactive disorder."

To resolve the majority of the problems in our generation, we only need to restructure the schools, the environment in which our children grow.

Dependence on Society

From very early on, we must pass on to our children our total dependence on society, for better or for worse.

On the one hand, we must show them through games, examples, and other forms that society can be very harmful. We must show how it overtakes and confuses people, and how it can actually "hypnotize" them to the point that if they follow it, they might find themselves behind bars the next day.

However, if they join a good society, its persuasiveness affects them positively.

These are the examples we must show children of all ages—in different ways so they will understand that by choosing their environment—the friends and the media they are exposed to—they are educating themselves and essentially determining their own fate.

From this we can conclude what we, as parents, must want the media to show, as well as everything else people are exposed to these days.

Conditions for Rearing a Human Being

E ducation means giving one the means to build oneself. If you want to build children by yourself, you are not building, you are forcing and coercing.

We must not tell them, "Do it this way and not another way." Orders are for taming animals, not for rearing human beings.

With a human being, you must explain, set up the conditions— an environment that consists of books, friends, and educators who will bring a child to the point of free choice in life.

This should begin at a very early age, before children are aware of what is happening to them. Even then, we must build around them situations from which they will learn, and through which they will educate themselves.

Only if a child is repeatedly impressed by the environment and receives from it the importance of the next step in one's growth will he or she be motivated to advance toward it and grow.

CHAPTER TWO
Balance with Nature

Part of the Whole

We

Must

Learn from Nature

Because

We

Are a part

Of it.

Wisdom of Life

All parts of Nature,
Inanimate, vegetative, and animate,
Coexist in perfect harmony,
In balance.

Man alone is out of balance,
Because his ego is ever erupting,
Forcing him to be,
The negative side of Nature.

If we learn how to balance ourselves,
How to rein in the evil,
And how to bond with Nature
In the right, integral way,
Out of self-awareness,
We will have a good life.

This is the wisdom of life
That we must teach our children.

Follow Nature's Example

The only right education
Is to follow Nature's example
Without believing
Or imagining,
Just as the wisdom of Kabbalah displays to us.

Our Lives Have a Purpose

The more we discover about Nature—the laws and connections within it—the more we see that everything is predetermined in a reciprocal, global connection on both the individual and the collective levels, just as all the elements in our bodies are mutually connected.

Accordingly, we must understand that our lives, too, have a beginning, a certain purpose we must ultimately achieve, and an end.

The Right Direction

We must adapt
Our internality
To the whole of Nature.

We must teach our children
How to bond
And how to love each other.
Without this
We will not survive.

If we pass on to them the right perspective on life, it will advance them and enable them to advance on their own. The important thing is to show them the right direction.

"Making It" in the 21st Century

In the 21st century,
One who "makes it" will be one who knows
How to treat others and the world favorably.

This type of person will succeed
Because he or she will be acting similarly to nature,
In balance with it.

Wherever you put such people,
You will find them not only surviving,
But thriving,
While others,
Those "hotshots" with all the money and savings,
Suddenly lose everything.

A Human Being Is One Who Wants to Bond

The general law of Nature
That operates on human society
Determines that people must be connected.

The wisdom of Kabbalah
Explains how to build a human being
Who wants to keep
That law of Nature within society.

The Scale of the Creator

"Education" means teaching a child what is more important in life and what is less so; what is good and what is bad; what is worthwhile and what is not.

Yet, what is the scale by which we measure education?

"A" is better than "B," not because it is better for me or you or anyone else, but because it is closer to the standard of the Creator—love and giving. This is the essence of education.

The Most Natural Is to Talk about It

Although it seems to us
That loving and giving
Are not in our nature,
They do exist within us.

When speaking to children about it,
We are not speaking to them about fictitious things
That humankind has invented in this world,
But about the foundations
On which the whole of Nature stands.

Similarity to the Creator

Adam [human being]
Comes from the word
Domeh [similar] to the Creator,
Similar to the upper force,
The force of Nature,
The quality of love and giving.

The transformation one experiences
Along the way towards it
Is called
"Education."

Free Development

The whole purpose
Of the wisdom of Kabbalah
Is to make us realize
That through one's own strength,
By individual decision,
And of one's own free choice,
One can become similar to the overall law of Nature,
Called "the Creator."

In contrast, there is nothing more
Opposite from evolution
Than trying to turn humans
Into machines
That merely follow orders
That we wish them to follow.

The Right Curriculum

We will not succeed if we make up study programs out of the figment of our imagination.

If our study programs do not go hand in hand with human nature, with the evolution of the world, and with all the systems that we live in, they are doomed to fail.

Therefore, the only solution is to read from the Kabbalistic sources that present to us the entire system of the worlds and explain where humankind should reach, where history, Nature, the evolution of society, and our own internal evolution are all leading.

In other words, first we must know which shape the next generation should take. Only then can we begin to contemplate the right way to prepare children for the conditions that will exist in their generation.

These conditions must be so clear to us that we can plan the steps by which we will usher our children into this future, perfect form.

Listen to Nature

We must be more attentive to Nature and take examples from it because Nature contains everything.

In the way that we approach people, in building society, in the proper shaping of the family, in the correct structuring of the environment for each of us, in the education at kindergarten, school, or university, in all of these we must look for answers in Nature.

The wisdom of Kabbalah, which is based solely on the study of Nature, says that if we take our knowledge from there, we will gradually achieve harmony with Nature. This is the only way to secure our well-being.

Going Along with Nature's Forces

The closer children become to the Creator,
The more they think in the direction He thinks,
The more they will succeed.
Why?
Because they will be flowing along with Nature's forces.

Two Things Every Child Should Know

1. There is Nature's inclusive force, a higher force that does everything, and we are under its governance.

2. If we wish to be happy we must make others happy, just like that higher force.

Children accept it naturally, and suddenly begin to see that the world really is arranged this way.

Adults, however, cannot understand it because they are already too complicated.

Today You Bite; Tomorrow You Are Bitten

We must explain to children
That we all want
Only to receive.
It is our nature.

But because our desire
Constantly pulls toward itself,
It causes harm to others.
And in the end,
This attitude comes back to us.

Today, you are biting.
But next time,
You will be the one bitten.
Isn't there a better way to behave?

Within Nature

In the end,
It is just a matter of
Teaching children
That they are within Nature.
This is the whole of education.

Grownups Change for the Little Ones

The minute we begin to treat children correctly, and wish for them to grow up in balance with Nature, we will be affecting Nature's system favorably, simply through our thoughts and wishes.

As a result, Nature's all-inclusive force will affect both children and parents, the entire system.

Thus, an educational system that is ostensibly oriented toward children will actually change and rebalance the grownups, too.

How? When grownups know, due to their responsibility and love for their children, that they must set a good example, they will be obliged to conduct themselves correctly for their children's sake. This, in turn, will change the grownups, too.

CHAPTER THREE
Example

A Child Learns from Examples

You can preach
A thousand times,
But research shows
That children do not hear.

They understand images.
They understand examples from life.
They look at what you do,
And learn from that.

Body Language

Children do not understand words.
They understand body language.

We must examine what we do:
Which movements,
At what pace,
With what look,
And with what attitude.
This is all that counts.

Children imitate us,
Like little fish
Follow bigger fish,
Precisely one to one.

Only Positive Examples

If you demonstrate an example to a child, that child will remember it for life, knowing that that's the way to behave.

"I want to be The Terminator," "I wish I were a mobster!" If these are the examples that they see, it's no wonder that this is what they want. Hence, the right approach is to always give them positive examples so that this is what they will aspire to become.

Until recently, we were concerned with showing children good examples through movies and stories. But the recent outburst of the ego has created a kind of deformity where the media has become the tool of education. And as for the media, only ratings count.

An Example for Life

We must provide children with positive examples
In all areas of life,
And the rest can be left entirely alone.

If the example is genuine,
And the child is impressed with it on a regular basis,
It will remain with him or her forever.

Formative Learning

We must expose children to various forms of conduct using films and plays. However, they can also decide for themselves to what extent they are okay or not.

Of course, the process should be accompanied by an explanation, analysis, and joint scrutiny of the matters by children and parents or educators. This is called "formative learning," which is how a person is impressed and learns.

CHAPTER FOUR
Games

Games Build a Person

A game is a serious thing.

Through it, a person grows.

A game builds the person.

A Way to Know the World

A game shouldn't be something designed to occupy children's spare time so they will leave us alone and play by themselves.

Children want to learn from games
They have a craving to know
To take apart, to break,
To do.

Children look at every moment in life
As an opportunity
To know the world.

Referring to games as "games" is our mistake. Children don't want merely to play; they want to understand as much as they can what lies behind everything, and how everything is connected.

Not Just Passing Time

A game to merely pass the time
Is something that satisfies us
Confused adults,
Because we want to pass the time.

Children have no desire
To merely pass the time.
To them,
The game is the way to know the world.

The Game of Life

Our whole life is a game because through games we develop.

Any growth in nature is carried out through play. Even the growth of cells is a game because they aspire to a future state that still doesn't exist.

Spiritual development, too, is a game.

And as for children, the "childish" games of every child determine the kind of person each of them will be.

Explanations Only Through Games

With children, we must never insist on something that is against their will.

Instead, we should explain to them what is good for them, what is acceptable for them, until, as Maimonides says, "They gain much wisdom."

They will gain wisdom through the explanations we will give them, but the explanations must come only by way of games. If we do it correctly, they will suddenly understand that it is not in their interest to remain in their present state.

Games of the New Generation

I would recommend building games for children through which they will see that one cannot succeed without the other children and that without them they would obtain nothing. This will teach them that...

Alone means weak,

Alone means small,

Alone means can't.

It is just like a team game: There is great competition, but it is nonetheless a game where everyone depends on everyone else.

Gradually, children will learn from these examples just how much they need society, and how much they can benefit from a good society if they return its goodness.

Games as a Means to Advance

The game needs to be an example, so the child will see that he or she is going up in rank.

In other words, what the child appreciated in the past becomes unimportant in the next state because something of a higher quality becomes the goal.

The Wisdom of Life in the World of Games

To bring children understanding
Of the essence of things,
We need to go to the level
Of those things that interest children.
How?
By revealing the wisdom of life to them
Through *their own* games.

Sophistication in Developing Games

For bonding, each party must make a few concessions. So the critical moment in a game should be when the child feels that:

> "I have to make a concession,
> But I *really* don't want to.
> But then
> If I give up a little,
> I'll succeed with the others!"

Success must specifically be with everyone, and not solitary. The expertise in developing games lies precisely in this point.

Growing through Effort

It makes no difference whatsoever
If children succeed
With the tasks we give them.

What matters is their effort
Because it is through their efforts that they grow.

CHAPTER FIVE
Teach the Boy "By His Way"

By His Way, Precisely to the Goal

"By his way" does not mean letting a child go wherever he wants, but leading him to the right goal by his way, meaning according to his level, his ability to perceive, and his character.

But the road still leads precisely to the goal.

Being Like the Creator

The rule: "Teach a child according to the child's way" means that we must maintain the child's qualities and merely offer a method that will help children put their uniqueness to good use.

From a state of exploitation of the entire world, a child must come to a state of "self-exploitation" to be similar to the Creator—loving and giving to others—while retaining his or her uniqueness.

By doing so, we bring up children to be like the Creator, but in their own ways. We provide them with the tools, and they do the rest themselves.

Nothing was created evil; it is all a question of how we approach it.

Inner Charge

We mustn't tell a child:
"Do it exactly this way" or "Do it exactly that way."
It is coercion.

Because in the end,
No one knows what inner "load"
A child inherited,
Which he or she must realize.

Each One Is Special

It is written, "There is no coercion in spirituality."

This means that each of us maintains his or her uniqueness in the human fabric, for without it we would not be able to complement the others in creating the inclusive picture.

Every person in the world is indispensable and none of us can attain perfection without everyone else.

We must treat the differences between us gently and respectfully because our traits were given to us by the Creator. All we need to correct is how we use them, without corrupting them and without oppressing ourselves.

This is the kind of education that the world needs today.

No Pressure

Do not pressure children;
Give them tasks that they can handle.

Know that many a wise man
Barely understood what was required of them at school,
And only when they finished school
Did they suddenly spring forward
And become great in their fields.

Don't Tell Them What—Tell Them How

The right way to educate is not to tell a child what to do. If a child asks, explain only how it should be done.

And what do you do before they ask? Use a variety of tactics to stimulate them into wanting to do what is right for them. The desire must come from the child. It may sound complicated, but it is the right way to educate.

The wisdom of Kabbalah opposes any kind of pressure. It explains that everything advances and persists only by man's will. What we must do is only to evoke the right desire.

Teach About Giving the Right Way

The wisdom of Kabbalah doesn't explain that giving is good, since this contradicts the child's desire.

You cannot tell a child something that contradicts the child's spirit and natural way. Instead, bring the child a game in which he or she will have to discover that it is better to treat others favorably, that one gains more by it, and that it pays off, meaning that it is rewarding because society encourages it and respects the child for doing so.

The positive attitude toward giving must be consistent. It is wrong to show a child that now we will treat him or her well after acts of giving, but tomorrow that response may change.

Children must learn that this is the truth of life, that it is Nature's way, and through the study, the change will occur within them.

The Way Nature Made You

One wants to be a musician,
Another, an engineer,
And a third dreams of being an electrician.
It is good that this is so.

As an educator,
I must build them into human beings
According to their abilities,
According to their qualities,
Which are preinstalled by Nature.

Put differently,
Instead of going against the Creator
Who created all those tendencies in children,
All those predilections,
I must help build them
As close as I can to *their* nature.

In the Direction of Love

"According to the child's way"
Means only giving a child direction.

B ut underneath, I must help the child realize that direction through the character he or she was born with, help them express themselves through everything that they received from Nature.

The important thing is that one's nature, the sum of one's qualities, be directed toward love and giving to others.

Every child is born with a special combination of qualities and tendencies. Leave it to them, but show them how they can use these qualities correctly.

Varied Explanations

We must offer as diverse explanations as possible and strive to give as many examples as we can, in as many ways as possible.

Sometimes it is very difficult to understand the teacher at school. But at home, with Mother or Father explaining things in a more suitable way, closer to the child, things become clearer.

This is how we should explain things to children: by using examples through which they can connect with the subject matter and thus learn more about themselves.

Division into Groups

As early as in elementary school, we can tell that children have their own direction. They sort it out for themselves, but we must help them.

Even as early as the first grade, a teacher can detect how each student perceives the world, relates to society, has likes and dislikes, and how they are built internally.

We should relate to children accordingly, dividing them into groups according to each one's unique nature: those who are more emotional, those who are more intellectual, and those who lean toward Nature, toward technology, or toward craftsmanship. Then we can explain everything to them, even the simplest things, according to that group's special tendency.

A Role in Society

We must provide every child with a role in society. That role must compel children to participate, to express themselves, and to carry out the group chores. Children must feel that they are in their own place.

Even the most aggressive children deserve that we find something constructive they can do in society. As a rule, we must find for the children occupations that will complement each of them within society.

Observing Oneself from the Outside

We must help children separate themselves from their nature.

We must tell them: "You see, according to your nature, you may be rude, stubborn, arrogant, or overbearing. But all that is not you; it is what's in you.

"Perhaps you can come out of that 'thing' inside of you.

"Let's try to change it together, and then you'll discover that you are changing your behavior toward everyone. This will be better for you, and you will profit."

Teaching children to distinguish between themselves

And the inclination within them

Is a great salvation for them.

In fact, it is the very basis of education.

PART THREE

At Home

CHAPTER ONE
Between Parents and Children

Being a Friend

A child should feel that a parent is a friend and big brother or sister, as well as a parent.

We must build relationships with children where there is trust, where the child welcomes the parent and wants them in his or her life.

Home

We don't understand how sensitive children are to the environment.

The mother should explain why she is going to work, why she is coming back, what her duties are at home, why relationships with relatives are the way they are, and why it is her duty do this and that, with any of the difficulties involved.

Likewise, a father should explain about his life.

Parents should also tell their children about all the joys that they derive from having them, how much care they are putting into them, and how much they enjoy them.

If parents convey all these things to their children, in the right measure, of course, not in the full magnitude and strength that they experience it, the children will be integrated into that feeling, and the atmosphere thus created will be called "home."

Avoiding Criticizing Children

Truth be told, we demand of our children what we ourselves couldn't achieve.

Because we're incomplete, we're trying to complement ourselves through our children.

This is why we sometimes put so much pressure on them.

The solution is to try to achieve wholeness by ourselves instead of demanding it from our children. This is precisely why the wisdom of Kabbalah was given to us.

If we achieve wholeness, or at least understand what it means and strive to achieve it, we will stop pressuring our children needlessly and will allow them to grow and develop as is best for them.

Order in the House

Question: How do you get a child accustomed to keeping order in the house?

Answer: If you don't accustom children to keeping order from very early on, if it doesn't become part of their nature, it will always be an effort until they throw those limitations behind their backs and flee.

The sooner we add discipline to love, the easier it will be for the child.

If we examine ourselves, we will see that we, too, are governed by pain and pleasure. We must explain to children that we are in a world that always works this way, and treats us in this way, too, and we should respond to it accordingly.

The Right Attitude Toward Grandparents

Parents must show their children the respect they have for their own parents, the child's grandparents.

By showing them how they treat their parents—grandma and grandpa—they are educating the child into treating them—mom and dad—the same way.

Self-Education

We must understand
That for our children's sake
We must
Educate ourselves
As well.

CHAPTER TWO
Between Siblings

Getting Along with One Another

Question: What do we do if siblings don't get along?

Answer: Find the common ground between them and constantly cultivate only that.

Find where they can support and help each other. That's the right way.

Siblings in the Family

We must explain to each of the siblings in the family that if they were born to the same parents and are growing up next to each other, then according to the soul, they are probably complementing one another and must be together.

They must understand that there is a bigger plan here, which made them siblings. Their family tie is precisely what allows them to complement Creation and relate to each other in a special way, building a mutual bond between them.

Such a bond doesn't let us say, "I don't want you to be; I'm pretending that you don't exist; leave me alone."

Every person complements the other, and in a family each member counts. Also, each new member has a place, regardless of tendencies or behavior—one may be reckless, the other indifferent, the third may like to daydream, and the fourth may be a rationalist.

Competition for Mother's Closeness

Question: How does one cope with envy and competition over the mother's closeness?

Answer: It doesn't depend on the children at all—only on the mother. Only she can position herself before them in such a way that they will be convinced that they are totally equal in how she treats them.

We learn that from the way the upper force treats us: One cannot attain the Creator unless connected through a bond of love to others, since the Creator appears precisely in one's connection with others. This is how a mother must present herself to her children: They will receive love on condition that they come to her with disputes together. And when they approach her separately, each of them will receive a slightly cooler response from her.

This way, she gets them used to cooperating in the right way, meaning that a truly warm response can be received only together. →

This kind of attitude builds within, systems that prepare one to be naturally inclined toward connection with others. Such people no longer see the goal itself, but ask from the beginning, "With whom can I achieve it?"

CHAPTER THREE
Parents

Demonstrating a Calm Relationship

From age zero to fifteen (at least), parents must display a calm relationship before the kids.

"Calm" means not changing drastically, not even for the better.

Parents must show their children that they are living a life of cooperation and mutual understanding, that the relationship between them is harmonious and calm without any abrupt and significant changes.

They also shouldn't display too much affection. Everything should be very solid and balanced.

Every Move Is an Example

The examples that parents give to children through the relationships between them will be passed on to their children's lives with their partners, and will exist in the families that they have.

We learn from examples and become educated by examples. We imitate everything we see during childhood. Therefore, we must present children with an image in which there are no problems.

An alcoholic father, a fight over something involving one of the parents' parents—a child will copy those examples and will search for them in his or her life.

Similarly, if there is something in common between the mother and the father, some inner bond that is higher than this life, and this is what keeps them together, the children will feel it. They feel that there is some sublime, yet solid basis that keeps their parents together above all that is happening.

No Fighting In Front of the Children

Fighting in front of the children is out of the question.
Home must be a place that is still, unchanging.
Confidence comes from home.
Quarrels between parents will shake up the children
And affect them in a very negative way.

CHAPTER FOUR
In the Family

Family Sessions

In a family, everyone is equal. No one is superior and no one is inferior.

A family is a place where everyone is in mutual love, and love can only be among equals.

"Equality" means that each family member has an opportunity to express an opinion. In response, everyone listens and consults with each other about it, and together all decide what is right for each member of the family depending on his or her age and situation.

When children regularly participate in such sessions, they calm down, knowing what goes to which person. They see that the family is working like a finely tuned, integral system.

The Family as a Small Society

Parents must build a small society together with their children, a society in which everyone makes concessions to the others for the good of the family. This good is greater than each family member's personal benefit.

By wishing to place the family's interests above one's own, family members will set an example for the other family members.

It's best if this can be done as a family game. This way, children will suddenly discover how much it can promote them, help them understand one another, feel satisfied, and enjoy how good everyone feels.

And what do you do if there is a child who is not willing to make concessions?

You must work with them with love, and thus strengthen everyone else. On the one hand, you need to show the child how much there is to lose because of unwillingness to put self second. But on the other hand, you can emphasize how much there is to gain if the child joins with everyone else.

It is best to do this at home, and to make sure that everyone plays together, as a family.

The Truth, and Nothing But the Truth

We must teach our children to speak the truth, whatever the truth may be.

Even when we see how selfish we are, that, too, is the truth, and we must be happy because it is the truth being revealed.

If we teach them that truth is a good thing—and truth is what a person feels within, whether it is "pretty" or not—then the child will immediately open up and stop thinking, "What will people think of me if I say this?" It will happen to them naturally.

A Single, Whole Body

Parents should relate to their child as a single body, not as two separate parents. The child mustn't see differences between the father and the mother. It is not good for children to believe they can "toy" with the mother's feelings.

It is true that we are talking about children's education and not about parents' education, but we must understand that everything is done through the parents, through the right environment. This could include the grandfather, grandmother, an uncle or an aunt—anyone in the child's vicinity.

It's very important that children do not feel any differences among those surrounding them. They must understand that everyone is treating them exactly the same.

Naturally, a child perceives a father and a mother differently, but parents must display a straightforward, sincere, proper, and equal approach toward every issue.

Equality in Regard to the Purpose of Creation

Children must feel
That we are teaching them how
To find their way in nature:

What is forbidden and what is permitted,
What is worthwhile and what is not,
What is dangerous and what is safe
In order to achieve the good end.

In this process, the parents and the children are together as one.

We are all one soul. As long as we are in this world, it is of no consequence whether you belong to this generation or to the previous generation.

Such an approach grants a child strength and confidence, a feeling that all are moving forward together, equal among equals.

Passing On the Precious

If something is precious to you,
You must pass it on,
Teach the children
About its essence.

A State of Love

Question: How do you tell a child about the spiritual world?

Answer: Very simply, tell the child that there is something superior to us that governs us. From that superior something, forces come down to us and affect us.

Why are these forces affecting us? In order to evoke within us a desire to rise back to that sublime, eternal, beautiful level.

This is how we will come to love each other,

Bond with each other,

And live as one man in one heart.

That state is called "the upper world" or "the spiritual world." This is the right way to explain it to a child. We must never lie to children; we should explain just a little, but only the truth.

Talk about Life

We must disclose
The meaning of life to children;
Tell them why they are here.

We mustn't fear that children won't understand what we are talking about. Even if it seems to us that they're not getting it, they are.

It's best to tell it using simple words, but it is highly recommended that we discuss with them the higher things in life.

PART FOUR
School

CHAPTER ONE
A System of Education

Life as School

"School" is a generic name for the process of our entire lives.

Regardless of how long we live, we are "at school" our whole lives.

If we look at our lives as an orderly sequence of changes whose purpose is to lead us into similarity with the Creator, then school is revealed in everything around us.

The "Wisdom of Life" School

At the "Wisdom of Life" school
You are taught how to be a "human being":

Why you were born,
What is happening in the world,
And what Nature is,
What stands behind visible Nature,
Why these forces affect us as they do,
And what we must do in response to that.

You are also taught
How you should relate to what happens to you,
How you are being treated,
And how you should treat others,
How to see life as a transparent image,
Disclosing the force that works behind the scenes,
And to truly be in touch with it,
as with a very close friend.

Such education guarantees that a child will make fewer mistakes, will not waste his or her life pursuing false goals, and will truly succeed in life.

The Purpose of School

The purpose of school
Is to build a global human being
Who behaves as a corrected element
In human society.

Such a person can set an example
For human society
Through one's behavior
And can lead human society
In everything humanity needs
In order to achieve perfection.

Separating Education from Literacy

Schools should make a clear distinction and separation between education and literacy. These two areas should actually be studied in separate buildings and taught by different people.

Of course, people who teach subjects like physics, mathematics, biology, and art should also set an example to students, and not just be experts in their fields.

To build a proper school, teachers need to be patient, experienced in their profession, and know how to combine the specific subject they teach with the child's overall education.

There is no such thing as mere learning. The student always follows the example of the adult, so the teacher should not only present the subject matter, but also show the impact of the subject on our lives. We must remember that although education and literacy are two separate realms, the emphasis must always be on education.

The Society Educates Its Members

W e should establish a school in which there is a different principle: society—the children's society—educates each and every child:

To be lenient,

Loving,

And to give to society.

In other words, the emphasis is on the environment. And to children, the environment is not the educators and the teachers; nor is it the grownups, but the children around them.

Therefore, if we prepare a good children's society around each child, a society that will condemn treating others badly and will praise treating others well, we will build a generation of children who behave differently.

A Destructive Framework

Question: Schools as we know them divide the day into lessons, breaks, homework, questions, answers, and so forth. Is this how they should be?

Answer: This type of education began only at the time of the industrial revolution, when workers were required to perform tasks on assembly lines. The purpose of education then was to qualify illiterate people to become factory workers. For this reason, the framework and the curriculum were set up to match the needs of the industry.

But today's children hate it because it runs against human nature. This system doesn't develop people, it destroys them.

No Ringing Bells

Question: At an ordinary school, the lesson begins and ends with the ringing of a bell. How should it be at the "Wisdom of Life" school?

Answer: There shouldn't be any bells at all in the school.

When the children and the educators decide together that the topic has exhausted itself, the lesson ends and the break begins. Then, during break time, the students can continue to discuss the issues that came up during the activity in the classroom.

Afterwards, a new lesson will begin on a new topic.

The lesson may take a quarter of an hour or an hour and a quarter, depending on whether or not the children and the educator feel they have to go further. In this way, people get used to being able to express themselves and work through the issues they are interested in to the full, without stopping in the middle.

Conversely, when there is an obliging timeframe, a person tends to shun responsibility and simply wait for the lesson to end.

When there is no timeframe, the child feels that the problem didn't disappear at the end of the lesson, but that he or she must still work it out, because we forever exist within the perfect nature.

That sensation makes one treat one's life differently. It builds within us a completely different approach to life—one that says, "I am in Nature and in my society, and I must resolve my problems by bonding with all the others."

Every Child Can

In class, children should not sit in rows, but in a circle. There, everyone is equal.

This principle should be sensed externally, as well. There should be no teacher in class preaching to the children, but a guide who is leading a discussion in which each of the students can express ideas and thoughts.

It cannot be that some of the children in class will be active and the rest will hardly be there or will only listen. The guide must allow each child to express him or her self as an individual, and everyone must be actively involved.

For example, the guide may read a story. Then, each of the children must comment on it: thoughts, feelings, opinions. It would also be good if each child wrote a few sentences about the story.

We should develop the special abilities that exist in each child without exception.

Learning Together

When the guide asks a question, children should help each other arrive at a common solution. In other words, they should constantly see that they are advancing as a result of mutual support. This foundation must be established before anything else.

Even later, when learning specific subjects, the guide must make the children discuss a certain topic and see that through their joint discussion, a common understanding arises. If one does not understand, another friend explains.

This is how the lesson should take place: You place a seed in the ground, such as a new bit of information about physics or mathematics. Then that seed is cultivated by the society through discussion among the children.

The environment develops from every idea, every piece of information, every approach, every sentence, and every decision.

Why We Learn

While studying the subjects, we should combine them with discussions about the meaning of life, to eliminate any difference between the topic and life itself.

Why do we learn geography, history, geology, mathematics, physics, or literature?

Why is the world built as it is, and why are its laws what they are?

In other words, we should explain to children the approach to each subject from within the overall reality.

While engaged in music, theatre, or sports, we should give children the sensation that these subjects were made to allow them to develop their senses to the maximum. Thus, they can determine where they are, where they are going, what they should feel in addition to their current feelings, and how they can grow as a result.

Developing a Human Being Through Discussions

Throughout history and until recent generations, all the children among the Jewish people could read and write, discuss the texts in the books, and perform analysis and synthesis.

The study method was unique—discussions: One person says this, but another thinks differently, and why is this so? Where is it coming from?

This is how you develop a human being—through dialogues and through difference of opinion.

Conversely, in the contemporary classroom there are hardly any discussions. Children are required to receive everything from the teacher and settle for it, memorize it, and most important—to pass the test.

No Development in Oppression

A person cannot develop through oppression.
With oppression, everything shrinks,
Closes.
This is the form of the current school.

We must teach children
How to develop themselves in the right direction,
With total freedom,
So the solution will always emerge from within them.

Look at how a plant grows,
How it detours around everything that blocks its way.
Nature finds the way to grow and to develop by itself.
Any oppression only harms Nature.

We must help children
Develop themselves without any limitations
And allow each of them
Internal freedom.

Observing the Entire System

A child who grows up with the wisdom of Kabbalah develops intellectual and mental capabilities that allow him or her to cope with anything, as well as to absorb vast amounts of information. For such a child, learning the sciences becomes easy.

Once a child receives an opportunity to observe everything from above and understand the general system, he or she immediately divides and arranges everything being taught—including science—according to their intrinsic patterns, applying the scientific approach they have acquired through the wisdom of Kabbalah.

The same applies to psychology and social sciences. These children control themselves, know where their drives come from, and there is nothing in the world that can stop them.

The Older Teach the Younger

In the younger age groups, children of different ages can be together part of the time, despite the great differences between them.

In principle, such conduct is very good for the younger ones among them because they take the examples of the older ones.

Children naturally aspire to be like the older children, so the older ones need to be properly educated on how to treat the younger ones, to guide them, and to teach them.

Integrating Children in Teaching

We needn't settle for a teacher's teaching. We should also use mutual help among the children.

The younger ones learn from the older ones, and the older ones, through their work with the younger ones, learn the right approach toward education and learning.

To an extent, the older children become teachers and gain insights about the way they themselves are being raised.

Young Educators

The wisdom of Kabbalah explains that only the adjacent higher degree can correct, educate, teach, and tend to the degree below it.

Although the mother is at a higher degree than her children, she must shift to a lower degree, though still a little higher than the child's, so she can promote the child little by little.

This is the way to advance that Nature has built for us. For this reason, it is best for the educators to be young and with a mentality and worldview that is as close as possible to the children with whom they need to work.

Educational Soup

Elements of internality should be integrated into all of the children's engagements throughout the day. This way, a child may play games, do sports, sing, dance, or eat, but still listen to discussions about the soul and study different topics.

The time at school should become a single whole, a "soup" that the child is in from morning until evening, one that concerns man and his world.

Children that grow in this way begin to view the world as a single whole, open to all the senses, to all channels, and this builds them.

Besides, in all those things, we must constantly integrate the work in the children's society, from the relations they develop among themselves to the approach they develop toward the world around them.

We must teach them to view reality in a broad, integral manner. A child shouldn't distinguish home from school, self from the world, or the perceptible world from the world beyond perception.

Instead,
Everything should be included within
As one whole.

This is called
"Love your friend as yourself."
When the child bonds with all the others
And feels that they are "his."

There aren't
Different topics,
A favored teacher or a hated one,
Friends he gets along with
And friends he does not get along with.

Nothing is divided,
But all is present now
To serve him.

A Single Picture

The wisdom of Kabbalah is the root of all sciences, the root of all teachings. When you begin to discover it, you discover in its light all the other teachings.

At the inanimate level, it is physics, chemistry, and geology. At the vegetative level, it is botany and ecology. At the animate level it is biology, zoology, and medicine. And then the speaking degree appears before you, which is what the wisdom of Kabbalah deals with.

However, everything must be tied into a single picture.

We split Nature into different disciplines when it is actually one whole. This is why we don't understand it. A child, however, perceives everything as one world, including the spiritual world.

Therefore, if we teach Nature as a single picture, without slicing it into disciplines, children will understand it better.

Shaping Children into a Group

In education, according to the wisdom of Kabbalah, each child is taught how to use the term "group."

It is like sailing—we arrive at the final destination only by mutual participation.

Children should be assembled into groups, not classes, and see that their education is done in a small society, or "a group," meaning "group education."

In other words, through practice, games, and other means, we should allow children to understand the meaning of the bonding of bodies that yields the bonding of souls.

Response from the Society

A ssume that a child did something bad in class.

The whole class witnessed it and began to condemn the child. They do not wish to speak with or accept the offender if he or she continues the same behavior.

Such an attitude from the society affects a child very strongly, and will prevent a repetition of the previous behavior.

Education, Not Punishment

Children need to determine their own punishments; otherwise, there is no education, just punishment.

Also, under no circumstances should the punishment be a result of our emotions at that moment.

We must relate to the incident only later, at the designated time for it, just like in court, where a case is noted on one day and discussed on another day.

When discussing it, we examine the ego that suddenly awakened in the child, like a little devil, causing the child to do bad things. The child needs to understand it and be aware of the common work we are conducting together in relation to what happens within us.

A New Kind of Reward and Punishment

Children should be treated in such a way that they understand the connection between punishment, reward, and the act itself.

They must understand that the punishment is not a punishment, but education. Similarly, positive feedback is not a reward, but a natural and correct result of the right action. Children must understand that whatever the case may be, the parents' and the educators' attitudes toward them are only for their best.

How should this be done?

The educator must create a situation where the child does not take the punishment as punishment, but as a kind of effect that will help him or her avoid a similar infraction in the future.

It is best to dedicate a special time during the week for discussing with the children everything that happened during the week.

For example: "Now you deserve this and that punishment. Would it be right to punish you this way? What do you think? Will such an attitude help you watch over yourself better next time, and avoid breaking the boundaries of behavior that we determined? Or do you think that a different kind of punishment is required? Let's think together; after all, we are working on your ego together.

"At the moment," you tell the child, "You are like an objective judge toward your ego. You and I are examining it from the side. What do you think we can do with this 'pest' inside of you?"

In this way, we educate and raise the level of the "human being" in the child. Otherwise, the child will misunderstand, become angry, and look for ways to escape punishment.

If we work correctly, the child will begin to see that we are treating him or her respectfully, as an adult—trying to find the best solution together to cope with the child's ego.

Seeing Life Correctly

We need to gradually build
A new approach to reality in children.

Instead of seeing life
As a competition with others,
We should look at life
As something to succeed with others.

This way, we will be able to spare our children
The problems of our generation.

School Begins at Home

The school should be close to what is happening at home. In other words, the parents, too, must be involved in the child's engagements at school.

> If at school they are discussing how to change,
> How to come closer to the purpose of creation,
> How to bond,
> The child should hear that this is the goal at home,
> And see that this is what is
> On the grownups' minds, as well.

That way, the child will not feel detached from the adult society and will not think such thoughts as, "When I grow up I'll do what I want. I just need to finish school and get out of here." Instead, the child will see that the grownup world is dealing with the same thing that the school is dealing with, and will appreciate it.

Therefore, it is very important that teachers, educators, and parents all be involved in the same inner work, the same process as the children.

Active Partner

The study
Must turn the child
Into an active partner,
Equal to the grownup.

Imagine what
Confidence and pride
Children will feel then.

Learning to Be Human

When the wisdom of Kabbalah teaches a person that he or she is operating solely on egoistic drives, it also teaches how one can transcend that egoistic nature and rise above the beast within to the human level.

It is a subject that can be taught at school.

A person who graduates from such a school will truly be human, and will know far more than how to read, write, and calculate.

CHAPTER TWO
The Guide

Let Love Rule

An educator is a person who was born that way.
It is a person who was born for friendship,
Not for domination.
An educator is one who feels that love should rule,
And not the educator.

According to the Boy's Way

Education should not be
According to the educator's way,
But according to the boy's way.

Otherwise,
Such a person cannot be an educator.

Seeing Far Away

A teacher must be
A person with very broad vision
And a very sound foundation.

Such a person must know where to lead the student, and to define what kind of students he or she wishes to see at the end of the process, after several years of working with them.

A Teacher = an Adult Friend

Question: How should students view the teacher?

Answer: As a grownup friend.

A teacher is not one who terrorizes and frightens, but one whose closeness the children want.

We needn't create a framework where children are told, "Get up!" or "Sit down!" as if they're in the military. Instead, there should be a friendly atmosphere in which children and teachers spend many hours together.

Bonding with Children

The guides must actually come down to the children,
And bond and mingle with them.

From within that state they should "toss around" some
questions so the children will work them out among
themselves.

But all scrutiny must be done within the group.

Understanding Children

To understand children, you must be at their level.

If you are bigger, then you're a teacher or a parent.
If you are smaller, you're a student.
If you are equal, you're a friend.

So if you want to understand children
And to bond with them,
You must be more like a friend.

Come Down to Bring Up

Guides need to come down to the children's level; that is, bond with them like friends. But while bonding, the guides should gradually change the behavior of the children.

They go to all kinds of places with the children, do all kinds of things with them, and behave like them. But at the same time, they gradually take the reins into their hands and design new modes of behavior in the children.

Together Toward the Goal

Children and parents must move together toward the same sublime goal, and not leave the teacher detached from the child's development.

The child must feel that the teacher is undergoing the same development and strives for the same goal.

Based on the teacher's own experience in walking that same road toward balance with Nature, he or she can disclose to children just a little more than what they already know. This should be the atmosphere while learning.

A Teacher is...

A teacher is one who teaches you
How to live,
How to survive,
How to understand the picture of the world.
A teacher is everything.
A teacher is the one
Who sculpts you
Into a human being.

Being a Teacher

In regard to the construction of a human being, to preparing children for life, only one who has developed in the spiritual sense of the word can be a teacher.

It cannot be a person who has just graduated from university or some other higher education institute.

How will that person teach the right conduct in the world if he or she still doesn't know what is happening within them?

A Role Model

The role of the educators
Is to provide the younger generation
With an example of the next degree
To which they should aspire
One step at a time.

Partners

If parents and teachers appreciate the goal
To which they are aiming the children,
They become partners,
Advancing together,
Evolving hand in hand with the children.

Education Begins with Attitude

Children develop by how they are treated,
By how they are spoken to,
And by the examples they see.

Therefore, a guide must set an example for the children
Through his or her attitude toward them
In every word,
In every action,
And in every movement.

"We create nothing new.
Our work is only to illuminate
What is hidden within."

Menachem Mendel of Kotzk

APPENDIX
Suggested Reading

The Wise Heart
Tales and allegories of three contemporary sages

The Wise Heart introduces a lovingly crafted anthology of tales and allegories by Kabbalist Dr. Michael Laitman, his mentor, Rav Baruch Ashlag (Rabash), and Rabash's father and mentor, Rav Yehuda Ashlag, author of the *Sulam* (Ladder) commentary on *The Book of Zohar*. The allegories herein provide a glimpse into the way Kabbalists experience the spiritual world, with surprising, and often amusing depictions of human nature, with a tender touch that is truly unique to Kabbalists.

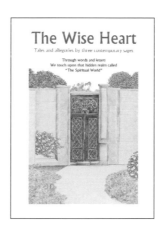

Together Forever
The story about the magician who didn't want to be alone

In *Together Forever*, the author tells us that if we are patient and endure the trials we encounter along our life's path, we will become stronger, braver, and wiser. Instead of growing weaker, we will learn to create our own magic and our own wonders as only a magician can. In this warm, tender tale, Michael Laitman shares with children and parents alike some of the gems and charms of the spiritual world. The wisdom of Kabbalah is filled with spellbinding stories. *Together Forever* is yet another gift from this ageless source of wisdom, whose lessons make our lives richer, easier, and far more fulfilling.

Miracles Can Happen
(tales for children, but not only...)

For children of all ages: ten enchanting tales that describe how *Miracles Can Happen* when we open our eyes to the joy and beauty that comes from being connected with others. This heartfelt collection of children's stories creates an appreciation for Nature's wondrous ways, revealing the eternal truth that only together can we do something truly wonderful.

The Baobab that Opened Its Heart
and Other Nature Tales for Children

The Baobab that Opened Its Heart is a collection of stories for children, but not just for them. The stories in this collection were written with the love of nature, of people, and specifically with children in mind. They all share the desire to tell nature's tale of unity, connectedness, and love.

Kabbalah teaches that love is nature's guiding force, the reason for creation. The stories in this book convey it in the unique way that Kabbalah engenders in its students. The variety of authors and diversity of styles allows each reader to find the story that they like most.

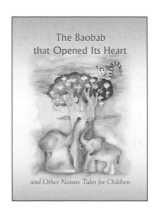

HOW TO CONTACT BNEI BARUCH

1057 Steeles Avenue West, Suite 532
Toronto, ON, M2R 3X1
Canada

Bnei Baruch USA,
2009 85th street, #51,
Brooklyn, New York, 11214
USA

E-mail: info@kabbalah.info
Web site: www.kabbalah.info

Toll free in USA and Canada:
1-866-LAITMAN
Fax: 1-905 886 9697